CONTEMPORARY SCENES
FOR YOUNG MEN
1985-2000

D0061573

CONTEMPORARY SCENES
FOR YOUNG MEN
1985-2000

Edited by Shaun McKenna

OBERON BOOKS
LONDON

First published in 2000 in association with the London Academy
of Music and Dramatic Art, by Oberon Books Ltd
(incorporating Absolute Classics)
521 Caledonian Road, London N7 9RH
Tel: 020 7607 3637/Fax: 020 7607 3629
e-mail: oberon.books@btinternet.com

A catalogue record for this book is available from the
British Library.

ISBN: 1 84002 141 1

Cover design: Andrzej Klimowski

Typography: Richard Doust

Printed in Great Britain by Antony Rowe Ltd, Reading.

INTRODUCTION

This collection of scenes for men contains material suitable for performers in their mid-teens and early twenties, and is ideal for auditions, festivals and LAMDA examinations. The range of material is wide and will cover LAMDA acting examinations from Acting Medallion right through to the Licentiate Acting Diploma. Each extract has been specially selected for its effectiveness and coherence as a scene in isolation from the play in which it originates. Every speech is annotated with notes on the character's age, situation, and any accent or dialect that might be required. The spelling and punctuation of the stage directions as well as the speeches themselves have been reproduced as they appeared in their original form. The date of the first performance or publication and the international standard book number have also been included.

Whilst the selections have been made with actors under the age of 25 in mind, this does not always mean that the characters fall into that age group. Some performers may wish to spread their wings and tackle something which might be out of their age-range. It is for this reason that some of the characters range up to their thirties. The collection, for ease of reference, has been divided into three sections, and the division has been made on the basis of the age of the character, not necessarily the age of the performer.

Contemporary plays often deal with controversial and sexual issues – and find expression in "bad language". This can present some difficulty for teachers looking for suitable material for teenagers. In this selection, these have been kept to a minimum, although some of the plays from which the speeches are taken may contain rather stronger material.

Shaun McKenna
March 2000

CONTENTS

PART ONE: TEENS

CROSSFIRE

by Michel Azama
(translated by Nigel Gearing)

Crossfire was first performed, in the original French, in Dijon in 1989. It was subsequently produced in the UK, in this translation, by Paines Plough in August 1993, at the Traverse Theatre Edinburgh and subsequently in London.

Crossfire *is a powerful play about war. Characters are caught in the crossfire both literally and metaphorically, as the issues that war brings up impinge on their lives and relationships and they tumble through the checkpoint between life and death.*

Yonathan is 15. He is a freedom fighter, in an unnamed struggle, who has just been killed by his former best friend, Ismail, circumstances having forced them to fight on opposite sides. He speaks to the audience.

Accent: any.

YONATHAN: The most difficult thing to do is cut the throat of a man who's still alive.

You mustn't waste a single slash of the knife and it's best to do it from behind.

Playing the hero is pointless.

We've booby-trapped cars doors cigarette-packets jerrycans stuffed with TNT we've fired fired fired even on kids because they grow up one day they'll shoot you in the back.

Helicopters dropped clusters of missiles the camp burned the vines burned across miles of hills stone-walls exploded.

It only takes 48 hours and then you're finished with the bombs the explosions the human pulp.

Hang on in there hang on in there just a bit further till the end

whole bunches of kids would throw themselves under the
tanks
they were crushed to death whole groups of them
others set on fire with flame-throwers
human torches still running for another hundred yards.

All for one more second of life.

Blood filling your hands clothes eyes walls.

Slaughter slaughter slaughter.

KERPOW! The other guy falls you step over him you
don't see anything any more you move forwards a corpse
falls on top of you explodes into bits and pieces all cut
to shreds and splashing you in a shower of blood.

At every step children in little bits babies their heads
burst open
disembowelled women holding on to their children
you're like an animal it's them or you
fire – bang! – at anything that moves a kid a cat a pal.

Bang bang bang save your skin bang bang bang bang.

He falls and does not move.

Available in *Crossfire*, published by Oberon Books Ltd.
Reprinted by kind permission of the publisher.

ISBN: 1 870259 34 3.

CROSSFIRE

by Michel Azama

See note on the play on page 11.

In this powerful play about the atrocity of war, 15-year-old Ismail and Yonathan have been inseparable friends. Now there is civil war, based on religion, and Yonathan is leaving to join the "other side". Ismail is talking to Yonathan.

Accent: any.

ISMAIL: Have you gone mad or what?

It's crazy. You were born here. We've always played soccer together. It's crazy.

No-one will hurt you here. You come from round here.

We're trapped. I feel lost. I try and understand what's going on. I listen to the radio. I try and keep up. This war's a war of lies. Everybody's lying. You can't know any more.

Wait. You can't just leave like that. We'll still see each other.

When we were kids the war was just a good excuse for bunking off school. You remember, we used to say: no school today! today's a bombing day!

You're my mate. My mate. One hundred per cent. I can't think of you as the enemy, it's impossible. I'd get killed for you here and now like a shot…Like a shot.

You remember you wanted to be a doctor and me an engineer.

On my fifteenth birthday we had a party, a picnic by the sea with some girls.

There haven't been any since.

Remember, that was the day it began.

For our picnic we had a barbecue. We danced with the girls. When we got back we didn't understand what that guy was saying. He was saying things are hotting up out there and when we got back…

I found my mother in tears. She thought I was dead.

We've spent our whole lives playing soccer and stealing figs.

You can't leave just like that. Over on the other side with the others. I don't believe you. Shooting at us. Shooting at me perhaps. I can't believe that.

You haven't a single real feeling in the whole of your body.

Available in *Crossfire*, published by Oberon Books Ltd. Reprinted by kind permission of the publisher.

ISBN: 1 870259 34 3.

YO-YO

by Dino Mahoney

Yo-Yo was first performed at the Warehouse Theatre, Croydon in April 1995 and was the winner of the 1994 South London International Playwriting Festival.

Lego is a disturbed 14-year-old boy from London. The play is set in a downmarket guest house at a Cornish seaside resort, during the August bank holiday weekend. Lego is staying there with his mother, who has left him alone for the weekend. He meets Kevin, a divorced teacher, who is hoping to spend some time with his own son. Lego, bored and lonely, forces Kevin to pay him attention.

Accent: London.

LEGO: Looked as if you could do with a bit of company, know what I mean. I ain't usually wrong. (*Silence.*) Been down here before?

Show you around if you like. Won't cost nothing. Go down the bird park. D'you like birds? (*Silence.*) Last week some kid smashed this bird's legs in with a cricket bat…flamingo …it was in the papers. Know what the RSPCA did? Took it off in a van and put it to sleep. Don't do that to cripples do they. (*Pause.*) So what's the plan for tonight?

Go down the Goose and Duck…lined up like skittles they'll be…scrubbers up one side, bikers down the other …leather boys, you know…creak when they walk. (*He mimes this with sound effects.*) What's hot, hard and throbbing and sticks out between your legs? (*Pause. LEGO mimes revving up a motor bike.*) Vrooom, vroom, vrooom…motor bike. Get it? You should see 'em at closing time…they do wheelies down the waterfront. (*Mimes rearing up and riding on the back wheel only.*) Vroom, vroooom…You can rent bikes down here…don't cost much. Ever been on one? Great ain't they. Rode over a badger once…didn't half hurt…bit me tongue.

D'you like fun-fairs? There's a great one down here…it's got a Rota…ever been on one? You know, you go in this room and stand up against the wall…then the door closes and the whole place starts going round really fast…then the friggin' floor disappears…ahhhh…(*He looks at the floor with all his fingers rammed into his mouth.*) but you're going so fast you're stuck up against the friggin' wall like a squashed fly…(*Pulls back his cheeks.*) G-Force… G-Force…and you've just scoffed a Big Mac, large french fries smothered in ketchup and a humungous chocolate milkshake…happened to this kid…threw the whole lot up…(*With flamboyant finger-wriggling hand gestures originating from the mouth outwards, he demonstrates how the kid threw up.*) Blaaaaaa. Looked like something out *The Exorcist*…(*Pressed up against the wall in a crucified position. In a deep, demonic voice.*) I am Beelzebub…(*He makes extravagant throwing up sounds with illustrative motions.*) You could see all these kids plastered up against the wall near him, (*Pulling his cheeks back.*) G-Force…G-Force… and this burgerpuke coming closer and closer…(*He mimes a tentacle of vomit approaching someone's face…and then reaching it.*) Ahhhhhhh!

Available in *Yo-Yo*, published by Oberon Books Ltd. Reprinted by kind permission of the publisher.

ISBN: 1 870259 50 5.

THE LION, THE WITCH AND THE WARDROBE

by C. S. Lewis
(dramatised by Adrian Mitchell)

This new adaptation of C. S. Lewis' famous Narnia story was first performed by the Royal Shakespeare Company at the Shakespeare Memorial Theatre, Stratford-upon-Avon, in November 1998.

Tumnus is a faun and therefore of no specific age. He has been included in the Teens section of this book as the role is likely to appeal to younger actors. The Kingdom of Narnia is ruled by the White Witch who keeps it in a state of perpetual winter and terrorises the inhabitants. A human girl, Lucy, has magically entered Narnia through a wardrobe and meets Tumnus. He has brought her back to his house where he has fed her and told her about Narnia. Suddenly he bursts into tears.

Accent: any.

TUMNUS: (*Sobbing.*) Oh – oh – oh! I don't suppose there's ever been a worse Faun since the beginning of the world. My old father, now. (*Points to the portrait over the mantelpiece.*) He would never have done a thing like this. I'm in the pay of the White Witch. She's the one who keeps all Narnia under her crooked thumb. She's the one who makes it always winter. Always winter and never Christmas; think of that!

I'm paid to be a – kidnapper. Look at me, Daughter of Eve. Would you believe that I'm the sort of Faun to meet a poor innocent child in the wood and invite it home to my cave for tea so that I could hand it over to the White Witch? But I have.

Don't you understand? It's not something I *have* done. I'm doing it now. You are the child. The White Witch told me that if ever I saw any human children, I must catch them for her. And you're the first one I ever met. So I pretended to be your friend and asked you to tea. And all the time I've been waiting for you to fall asleep so I can go and tell *Her.* If I don't, she's sure to find out. She'll cut off my tail, saw off my horns and pluck out my beard. And she'll wave her wand and turn me to stone and I'll be a statue of a Faun until the four thrones at Cair Paravel are filled – if that time ever comes.

I didn't realise what Humans were like. But now I know you, I can't hand you over to the Witch. If I see you to the lamp-post, can you find your own way back to Spare Oom and War Drobe?

Available in *The Lion, the Witch and the Wardrobe*, published by Oberon Books Ltd. Reprinted by kind permission of the publisher.

ISBN: 1 84002 049 0.

THE LION, THE WITCH AND THE WARDROBE

by C. S. Lewis
(dramatised by Adrian Mitchell)

See note on the play on page 17.

Aslan is a mystical lion and therefore of no specific age. He has been included in the Teens section of this book as the role is likely to appeal to younger actors. Aslan is the spirit of goodness who has returned to Narnia to defeat the chilling power of the White Witch. He is talking to Peter, Susan and Lucy, as well as his supporters in Narnia. He has just agreed to sacrifice himself to save Edmund's life.

Accent: any.

ASLAN: You can all come back. I have settled the matter. She has renounced the claim on your brother's blood.

His people cheer. ASLAN silences them by raising a paw.

There is work to do. You must move from this place at once, for it will be wanted for other purposes. We will encamp tonight down there at the Fords of Beruna. As soon as she has finished her business on this hill, the Witch and her crew will fall back to her House and prepare for a seige. You may be able to cut her off in the wood. Now if you fight the Witch and her creatures there, you should use your main force to drive down from the high ground. But keep your Centaurs below the wood, ready to charge when the Witch is chased out.

On the other hand, if you have to assault her castle, surround it at a distance, move in gradually, wait and watch until you find her weak point.

Will I be there myself? I can give you no promise of that.

(*In a dull voice.*) She will not attack tonight. (*He sighs.*) All the same, that is how a soldier ought to think. But it

doesn't really matter. Come now, Peter, let us join the
others at the Fords and take our supper together.

Available in *The Lion, the Witch and the Wardrobe*, published by
Oberon Books Ltd. Reprinted by kind permission of the
publisher.

ISBN: 1 84002 049 0.

FAITH

by Meredith Oakes

Faith was first performed at the Royal Court Theatre Upstairs in October 1997.

The play is set on a small island. A group of soldiers are fighting for possession of the island, but nothing in their training prepares them for the dilemmas they face. Lee Finch is 19 and a private in the army. His faith is to be ready to die. He, together with his sergeant and other soldiers, have been billeted on the unwilling Sandra, to whom he speaks here. Sandra has just asked him why he has given his sergeant a hard time.

Accent: London.

LEE: He's a sergeant, isn't he. Sergeants are so boring, everyone hates them. Everyone hates them 'cause everyone wants to be mad. And sergeants want to be sane. They want to be sane so badly. They wind up being madder than all the rest of us put together.

No, this is it, they have an impossible task because they have to train us. They have to train us to be hard, see, which means they have to be hard on us. There was one used to get me up five o'clock every morning my first three weeks. Out running before the sun came up, all round the barracks with ice all over the roads and they'd be shouting at us how we were the worst they'd ever had, so weak, no puff, they were all day telling me how thick I was and I'd never make it, it's just, I like to stop and think but you're never supposed to, so they're all the time making out I'm a halfwit because I have thoughts.

They break you right down, they make sure you know exactly how bad life can be when they don't respect you, nothing you do seems to please them and they make you feel like a boil on the face of the earth. Then one day you do something right and someone gives you a good word suggesting they don't hate you quite as much as before. So then the joy of living starts up again, it's like you're born again and they've become your parents, a few weeks down the line and by then you're well in. You're not allowed home the first six weeks. They know what they're doing see. By that time they've become your family, you've won the acceptance and you're really happy they let you belong. Only that's when it comes as a bit of a shock when they let you go off and get killed, because families aren't supposed to be like that.

But this is the sergeant's problem. Because the reason he takes the trouble to be hard on you is that he cares. The more he cares, the more he treats you like a bastard. The more he treats you like a bastard, the more he cares. I don't think it's good for them. They get really strange, some of them. They get really nice to you. It's horrible.

Available in *Faith*, published by Oberon Books Ltd. Reprinted by kind permission of the publisher.

ISBN: 1 870259 80 7.

PART TWO: TWENTIES

SUGAR SUGAR

by Simon Bent

Sugar Sugar was first performed at the Bush Theatre in July 1998.

The play is set in a guesthouse in Scarborough, in winter. The guesthouse is run by Val who was 'a bit of a goer' in her youth. Her family, like her establishment, is in disrepair. Then an enigmatic visitor arrives – Dennis Wilson – and brings a sexual charge that electrifies the household and threatens to tip it over the edge. In this scene he is talking to Val, who is upset because of her son's deteriorating marriage. Here, Dennis is consciously identifying with her inner feelings, making himself ever more sympathetic. The delivery is almost hypnotic as he works his unusual seduction technique.

Accent: any.

DENNIS: You need a cup of tea. I've put the kettle on.

He pours a large glass of dandelion and burdock and drinks it in one.

I know that something good or bad is happening, that it's about to happen and that I'm not where I should be…I forget everything – years, people, days…gone, dissolved…trembling – the walls close in…my heart trembles – I sit, I smoke, I stand, walking with fear, shaking, every breath is my last – each cigarette lasts a lifetime, an eternity to smoke – I don't smoke – I get the fear, I get the fear and there's nothing – it's all nothing and I cling on for the light, if it's still the same, if it hasn't gone – in the morning, in the cold clear light of day…dissolving – every day and I feel like a foreigner…I can't remember.

It's alright when I'm lying down. I lie awake at night with my eyes open…a loving mother, a loving father, a loving woman to wrap their arms around me…in the end I wrap my arms around myself…and I start praying …'Oh dear Lord'…'Please dear Lord' – and I can't get up and I think everything would be alright if only I was dead and I don't want to die and then I get up. I can't think of anyone.

You're not stupid.

No, you're not.

I bet you were a very attractive young girl. A very very attractive girl.

Tell me you're a very attractive woman. Say it.

Of course you can. A very attractive woman.

That's right.

Available in *Sugar Sugar*, published by Oberon Books Ltd. Reprinted by kind permission of the publisher.

ISBN: 1 84002 033 4.

THE DARKER FACE OF THE EARTH

by Rita Dove

The Darker Face of the Earth, by the USA's former poet laureate, was first performed at the Oregon Shakespeare Festival in July 1996 and in the UK at the Royal National Theatre in August 1999.

The play is set in South Carolina, in the Southern United States, in the 1840s. The action takes place on the Jennings Plantation. Twenty years previously, Amalia Jennings gave birth to a son by a black slave. The child was smuggled out of the plantation. Now the charismatic slave Augustus, of mixed parentage, has come to the plantation. Augustus is a tall, handsome young man with caramel-toned skin and piercing eyes, his righteous anger thinly concealed behind his slave mannerisms. He is speaking to Amalia, with whom he has a challenging relationship.

Accent: *Southern American.*

AUGUSTUS: Now I have a story for you.
Once there was a preacher slave
went by the name of Isaac.
When God called him
he was a boy, out hunting ricebirds.
Killing ricebirds is easy –
just pinch off their heads.

Indicating the sherry.

May I?

AMALIA flinches, nods. He pours the sherry expertly.

But one day, halfway up the tree
where a nest of babies chirped,
a voice called out: 'Don't do it, Isaac.'
It was an angel, shining
in the crook of the branch.
Massa let him preach.
What harm could it do.

Sitting down in the damask chair.

Then a slave uprising in Virginia
had all the white folks
watching their own niggers
for signs of treachery.
No more prayer meetings, Isaac!
But God would not wait,
so Isaac kept on preaching
at night, in the woods.

Of course, he was caught.
Three of his congregation
were shot on the spot, three others branded
and their feet pierced.
But what to do about Isaac,
gentle Isaac who had turned traitor.

First they flogged him. Then
they pickled the wounds with salt water,
and when they were nearly healed,
he was flogged again, and the wounds
pickled again, and on and on for weeks
while Massa sold off Isaac's children
one by one. They took him to see
his wife on the auction block,
baby at her breast.
A week later it was his turn.
His back had finally healed;
but as his new owner led him
from the auction block,
Isaac dropped down dead.

Pause; more to himself than AMALIA.

They couldn't break his spirit,
so they broke his heart.

Available in *The Darker Face of the Earth*, published by Oberon Books Ltd. Reprinted by kind permission of the publisher.

ISBN 1 84002 129 2.

WITTGENSTEIN'S DAUGHTER

by Dic Edwards

Wittgenstein's Daughter was first performed at the Citizens Theatre, Glasgow in September 1998.

The play is a serious comedy concerning Alma Wittgenstein, daughter of the influential philosopher. Bored by her neo-fascist husband and the threat he poses to her values, she goes to Cambridge to investigate the ideas of her late father. Here she meets one of her father's old friends, the 100-year-old ex-boxer, Beckett. Here, Beckett appears as he was when he first met Wittgenstein, as 21-year-old Young Beckett, a boxer. He talks to the audience.

Accent: *Cockney.*

YOUNG BECKETT: I like telling the troof. I'm an 'omosexual. Me. Terry Beckett. Boxer. Age 21. I don't mind 'oo knows. Warr annoys me is, I come to these parties regular. I get into 'em cos I'm an 'omosexual. Only tonight, the bloke at the door didn' wannit. Didn' wanttu let me in. So he puts on that voice: you know: I'm fwightfully sowwy. Meaning: you can't fuckin' come in. And you will find up and down this land that speaking like that counts. But iss like a game. Just keeps you duckin' and divin' all ovu the place. Iss part of their weapons, those words like jewels in the 'andle of a ceremonial dagger. And you can't get past their words in frough the door. (*He hits something.*) You see 'em in their bit of town round King's Parade all the toffs, the students. That's why they call it that cos they're all aparading like kings but the townies don't like 'em and you can't blame 'em, they was 'ere first, the townies. Iss like the townies are just there tu serve the toffs. Get 'em into our bit of town and you can serve 'em wiv an uppercut. (*Uppercuts.*) So I says: I know you can stop me comin' in because wiv that voice you got the auffowity. *But* can you wiv that voice tell the trooff? Can you wiv

that voice say: I am an 'omosexual? And I know that 'e
is 'cos it's an 'omosexual's party and 'e's on the fuckin'
door! So I says: I can. I can say it. I am an 'omosexual!
Wiv that they let me in! Then I meet this bloke quite
quickly and we come up to this room and 'e shuts the
door and immediately 'ides down by the side of the bed!

Available in *Wittgenstein's Daughter*, published by Oberon Books
Ltd. Reprinted by kind permission of the publisher.

ISBN: 1 870259 35 1.

SUSAN'S BREASTS

by Jonathan Gems

Susan's Breasts was first performed by the English Stage Company at the Royal Court Theatre Upstairs in May 1985.

The play concerns the difficulties of love among a group of successful twenty-somethings. Lemon is 24, good-looking and muscular with long hair. He has rich parents and is decidedly eccentric in both dress and manner. He is talking to Susan, with whom he is obsessively in love. Previously he has kidnapped her and as a result has been committed to a psychiatric hospital by his parents. Susan is an actress. A doctor told her she was sterile but she now finds herself pregnant.

Accent: any.

LEMON: I love you. Let's get married. Course I'd have to get out of Whitecroft first. I need you to help me do that. And then, as soon as I'm declared sane we'll have lots of money…'cause it was my twenty-fifth birthday recently, so I've got my grandfather's money to pick up. The inheritance. But I have to be sane to get the money. It's in the terms of the trust. And then we could hit the road. Travel. Go anywhere. Have the baby in Italy or Venezuela or Connecticut. Get away from all these nazis everywhere.

It'll be great! What's the matter? All we do is, first, get me out of that dump, then…Look, would you mind if we don't get married in a church? I hate churches. What I'd really like is to get married in the woods. There's a place near where my granny lives. Near Bournemouth. Primrose Wood. It's a completely magical place. There are actually fairies there. I've seen them.

What's the matter? Are you alright?

Oh well, we don't have to get married. It's stupid marriage anyway, isn't it? We love each other, that's what

matters. And we're going to have a baby. It's a miracle.
So, I'd better start behaving myself. The trouble is I'm in
there with a whole lot of complete loonies. It's a bad
atmosphere. And they keep giving me drugs. I'm caught
in a trap.

My parents had to get me certified. They had to. It was
either that or go to prison. I've behaved incredibly badly
towards them. Especially my father. I don't know why
because really the only evil thing they ever did to me
was to send me to public school. But, Susan, if we could
get married and leave the country, we could be so happy.
You and me together. Start afresh.

SUSAN begins to shrink away from him.

I think about you all the time. I dream about being with
you in the desert, in the jungle, in the mountains – all
sorts of places. I dream about getting a house with you.
I can see it. Like the Dulux commercial. Lots of bright
sunshine and white paint. And filling you up with babies
and surrounded by dogs and cats and birds and hens
pecking in the yard. Domesticity! Accomplishments!
Making a hen-house. Putting new spark plugs in the car.
Scraping the carrots, earning a living. Whatever we have
to do.

Available in *Jonathan Gems: Three Plays*, published by Oberon
Books Ltd. Reprinted by kind permission of the publisher.

ISBN: 1 870259 10 6.

PERPETUA

by Fraser Grace

Perpetua was first performed at the Birmingham Repertory Theatre, in association with Soho Theatre Company, in April 1999.

In the town of Pensacola, Florida, a battle between an abortion clinic and an extreme pro-life organisation comes to a head, pitting the law of God against the law of the land, and the right to life against the right to choose. John is a volunteer worker at Father D's extreme pro-life organisation, Operation Freedom. He is described as having a non-threatening build and being quietly good-looking. He is talking to Angela, one of the organisation's key workers.

Accent: Southern American.

JOHN: Angela. Can I ask you a question? 'Bout Father D. I'm not quite sure how ta put a question like this. You ever think Father D's kinda different from us? I don't mean cause he's black…I don't. Now I met him, Father D's even more than what I thought he was. All full of joy an' stuff. He's got all the words an'…there's so much in him God can use, fer what we're fighting for. I'm not juss puttin' a downer on myself before yer say it. There's things I can do, I'm not ashamed to admit that. I know cars, I know guns, I know a few other things. Nothin' seems ta fit.

I mean I can do other things, I can do posters an' park pick-ups all day, but thass not really who I am, Angela. Am I makin' any sense?

See God's only spoke ta me twice in my life. Like twice I know fer sure. One time it was this thing 'bout what I got ta give, that He could use it. Th'other time was listenin' ta this song. Real old song, by the Beach Boys, Bee-gees someone like that. You know the one?

It goes, the pen is mightier than the sword, but no match

fer a gun. Sometimes I'd sit up there in Akron, tearin' off all these stamps I'm s'posed ta be stickin' on, thinkin' how every one a them is one a the unborn that'll die taday. I'd juss think a those words. Do you think there'll ever be a season – I don't mean now – I mean, the way things are goin', d'you ever think there'll be a season for people like us? People who don't have all the gifts. Gifts a eloquence and wisdom…

Ah'm sorry. I blew it. Lord Jesus I messed up big time.

Available in *Perpetua*, published by Oberon Books Ltd. Reprinted by kind permission of the publisher.

ISBN: 1 84002 122 5.

SOUNDS...IN SESSION

by Tyrone Huggins

Sounds In Session was first performed by Theatre of Darkness in 1998.

The play is set in a recording studio during one night as Nic, Tanya and Tony come together to record the final track of a compilation album. Tony is black, a social worker by day and an old school friend of Tanya's. He has resisted being exploited by the music business by keeping his day job but has a skill with computer-sampled music which the other two need. The author writes, 'At night in his bedroom he unlocks inspiration from his computer-based sound system, creating music in the ether that nobody hears. This is his first exposure to the manipulative world of the biz.' During the course of the session, the three have smoked a lot of cannabis.

Accent: *Black London.*

TONY: This is getting interesting now. Chemistry then. Between a man and a woman, the way you tell it. But it comes in here as well. (*Holds up spliff.*) In this. All the drugs we consume. You've been drugging yourself up to the gills all night.

This isn't about comparison. I use a different cocktail. We all do. That's what really rubs up the belly of this united white man's kingdom. Who controls them.

No, not so simple. On to the why. Why they will have to accept this, one day. (*Holds up spliff.*) You see, I wasn't brought up on this stuff. Here. (*Passes joint.*) My parents would dispossess me. But they don't understand the social, the economic purpose of it. That's another subject I learned on the Open University. They should ban it. Information is power. That's the thing about the internet. The reason they'll legalise this is because they'll have got control of it. It is simple, isn't it? They'll have wrested control of it from the hands and the minds of those to whom it is indigenous. They will have worked out what it does. With their chemistry sets. Like tea from China – India. Coffee from Brazil. Diamonds and uranium in South Africa. King sugar in the Caribbean. All drugs in their own way. What is a drug? Something to make you feel better? The nuclear deterrent?

Capitalism was also invented before I was born. Is that about morality? No. It's about commodities. Things to be owned, controlled, enslaved. Sometimes I think I only smoke spliff as a form of protest. But it's more important than that. It keeps my mind operating differently from yours. I'd hate to think the way you do. To see the world with your mind-set; your thought-patterning – mind set in stone.

Available in *Sounds…In Session*, published by Oberon Books Ltd. Reprinted by kind permission of the publisher.

ISBN: 1 84002 096 2.

PLAYING SINATRA

by Bernard Kops

Playing Sinatra was first performed at the Warehouse Theatre, Croydon in October 1991.

The play concerns an obsessive, exclusive brother-sister relationship between Norman and Sandra. Norman is an agoraphobic bookbinder who is obsessed with the life and music of Frank Sinatra. Their lives are changed when Phillip de Groot enters Sandra's life and threatens to tear Norman and Sandra apart. Philip is a charming, good-looking, open man who smiles a lot. His voice is soft and gentle. He always listens and never interrupts.

Accent: *any.*

PHILLIP: I am a seeker. I used to be an architect. Not bad. Mainly hack work; the exigencies of modern life. The realities. The compromises one has to make. Then one day, whilst walking in China. I was walking along the Great Wall actually, when I had a kind of mystical experience. It was if you like my Road to Damascus. An inner voice boomed. Phillip de Groot! What are you doing with your life? What was I doing indeed? From that moment on I was plagued with inner doubt. What is the meaning of me? What is the meaning of existence? Is there a meaning? Should there be a meaning? *Qui somme-nous*? *Ou allons-nous.* The binding is the person, indeed. But my binding fell away. I was terrified. I almost fell apart.

Sandra gives him a biscuit.

Ginger snaps. How very nice. How did you know these were my favourites? Anyway, I survived that greatest crisis in my life. And I chucked it all in. I dabbled in many things, trying to find my new self. I've travelled extensively in India. Did voluntary work among the bereft of Africa. All the time questioning, surviving. You see me as I am, a seeker. I believe we are the stuff that dreams are made of but we, man, humankind, is in terrible danger. And we are the danger. I have a modest income. A legacy. I am content, yet not complacent. I am still searching for my true vocation. I hope that answers your question.

Available in *Bernard Kops: Plays One*, published by Oberon Books Ltd. Reprinted by kind permission of the publisher.

ISBN: 1 84002 071 7.

THE COLOUR OF JUSTICE

edited by Richard Norton-Taylor

The Colour of Justice was first performed at the Tricycle Theatre, Kilburn in January 1999 and subsequently on TV and at the Royal National Theatre.

The play is based on the harrowing transcripts of the Stephen Lawrence public enquiry. In 1993 black teenager Stephen Lawrence was stabbed to death in a racist attack by a gang of white youths. The police investigation failed to produce sufficient evidence to convict. Here, Duwayne Brooks, a young black Londoner and contemporary of Stephen, now in his early 20s, tells of the night of the murder and his experience afterwards.

Accent: *Black South London.*

DUWAYNE: On the eighth of May, I went to a large anti-racist demonstration outside the British National Party headquarters in Welling. I went to protest against Steve's murder and the way the police were handling it. In October 1993, I was arrested and charged with offences arising out of the demonstration. They waited until the Crown Prosecution Service had decided to drop the prosecution against the killers. It was devastating. It felt like the police and prosecutors decided to get at me to ruin my reputation – and the chance to get any future prosecution for the murders. But the judge at Croydon Crown Court wasn't having any of it. In December 1994, he stopped the prosecution saying it was an abuse of the process of the court.

I think of Steve every day. I'm sad, confused and pissed about this system where racists attack and go free but innocent victims like Steve and I are treated as criminals and at the outset ignored me when I pointed out where the killers had run and refused to believe me that it was a racist attack.

I never knew Steve to fight no-one. Steve wasn't used to the outside world. He wasn't street-aware of the dangers of being in a racist area at night-time. I shouted to run. He had ample time to run as the boys were on the other side of the road. Steve didn't understand that the group of white boys was dangerous.

I was taken to the identification parade. I saw a skinhead there, Stacey Benefield. He said the boys who stabbed him were known to stab people and not to get done for it. He said they knew people in the police. I now know that the person I picked out was Neil Acourt.

On the third identification parade, I now know I identified Luke Knight. Sergeant Crowley said something to the effect that I was guessing. I got angry. I recognised the attackers from the attack and not from any outside information. Nobody described the Acourt brothers to me. I did not know how important Sergeant Crowley's lies were until I heard it on the news that the two men who had been arrested had been released and it was to do with my evidence not being good enough.

Available in *The Colour of Justice*, published by Oberon Books Ltd. Reprinted by kind permission of the publisher.

ISBN: 1 84002 107 1.

THE NEIGHBOUR

by Meredith Oakes

The Neighbour was commissioned by the Royal National Theatre Studio, and first performed at the Cottesloe Theatre in April 1993 as part of the Springboards Festival.

The play is set on a London council estate where two young men, John and James, who live next door to each other, suddenly become enemies, invoking destructive forces beyond their control. The community takes sides like spectators cheering from a grandstand as the conflict escalates into tragedy. Here James is talking to Stephi, the young woman with whom he lives, and his sister, Liz.

Accent: *London.*

JAMES: You're far more interested in me than I am in you. But then, what's there to know about you? Do you think I feel jealous? I don't. That's how predictable you are. I see you with someone else, it don't bother me.

    Next time you're talking to your friend next door, remember to thank him for destroying my credibility. I'm skint, ain't I. I'm unemployed. I'm going to have to live off you from now on, and you can't even afford to keep me in this hairstyle. What you being so quiet for? Tired are you. You ought to get a better job. Since you been out cleaning your hands are like alligator paws. They ain't soft like they used to be.

    This ain't the first time that things have gone wrong for me. But I'm lucky. My enemies go down and I survive. You want to know what I'm capable of. I'm capable of anything. What you want me to do? You want a demonstration. What you doing with the kettle, Liz? Give it here. Come on, give it, it ain't yours. Now watch this, Steph. I'm going to throw it on you, look.

Makes as if to throw it. LIZ screams.

Don't you trust me? What you take me for? You got
a high opinion of me, ain't you. I can't make you out.
You're living every day with someone who puts you in
fear. It's unbalanced.

Available in *The Neighbour*, published by Oberon Books Ltd.
Reprinted by kind permission of the publisher.

ISBN: 1 870259 31 9.

THE EDITING PROCESS

by Meredith Oakes

The Editing Process was first produced at the Royal Court Theatre in October 1994.

The play concerns the editorial staff of a small magazine, Footnotes In History, *which is taken over and, effectively, consumed by a large multi-national publishing house. Despite assurances to the contrary, the knives are out for the existing editor of* Footnotes. *His staff soon find themselves manipulated and even redundant. Ted, 29, is a writer, scholarly by nature, working on a biography but financially dependent on his job at Footnotes. Lionel is the general manager of the parent company. Ted will do anything to get into Lionel's good books, including having sex with him.*

Accent: *any.*

TED: (*To audience.*) By nature I'm far from being a leader. I'm scholarly. Months ago I made the decision that everything has to come second to my biography of Guizot. Unfortunately, not being privileged with a grant of any kind, I'm dependent for my livelihood on this snotty, half-baked magazine. I'm squandering my best energies and the shame of it makes me cringe, but the reason I cringe is in order to protect my better self and keep it in reserve until the time has come. It would be wrong to take my cringing for weakness. If a scholar, sitting over his biography of Guizot, hears a noise from outside and realises he's under attack, naturally he'll defend himself. He'll come blinking out into the light and give as good as he gets in defence of his peace of mind and of his work, which will just have to wait until he's properly secured his position. As editor of *Footnotes in History* I'd be in a better position to take time off, possibly I could get help with airfares to Belgium. Even if I'm not by nature a leader.

To LIONEL.

I feel I've been used. You've been avoiding me. I'll help
you. You need a deputy. I feel you don't respect me. As
far as you're concerned I'm just beefcake. Prove me
wrong. Make me your deputy.

Because you've told me yourself, publications are being
terminated all the time here, so what I really need is to
become part of the permanent management structure and
then my position would be more secure. Wouldn't it?

I think that is the point. It's true I'm first and foremost
a scholar. But scholars will only be respected if they're
seen to hold their own in the marketplace. I know a lot
about Guizot's views on the development of the
monarchy in Europe. Are you saying my knowledge is
irrelevant? Guizot has some interesting things to say
about periods in history when selfish forces are let loose
and when egotism prevails, either through ignorance and
brutality or through corruption. At such times, society,
plunged into conflicts of personal will, and unable to
summon any will to the common good, passionately
desires strong guidance by a sovereign, so as soon as any
institution displaying sovereign characteristics appears,
people flock to it, Guizot says, like condemned men
seeking sanctuary in a church. I think we can agree that
a company is a sovereign institution. A company such as
this one is a bulwark against social collapse. I'd make it
my aim to promote company loyalty.

You think I'm joking.

Available in *The Editing Process*, published by Oberon Books
Ltd. Reprinted by kind permission of the publisher.

ISBN: 1 870259 46 7.

FAITH

by Meredith Oakes

See note on the play on page 21.

Private Mick Pike is a soldier, aged 20, stationed on an island somewhere in the South Atlantic during a time of war. He is talking to his comrade in arms, Lee.

Accent: any.

MICK: The way I look at it. An order which is so obviously questionable has to be, by definition, an order that was made with very good reason. It's not as if they like making questionable orders. So obviously if he finds he has to make an order like that, such an obviously questionable order, the last thing he wants is for anyone to question it.

The problem with something like this. A questionable order like this. We assume it results out of careful deliberation. We assume there are special circumstances. We assume that all the careful deliberation which people have been doing for years has finally resulted in someone having the right to make this questionable order in special circumstances.

Of course all the time it might just have come from some twat.

I haven't thought about anything back home since we got here. How many people back home have ever been tested. How many of them would be ready to die for their faith. What's your faith Lee.

Being ready to die? Is that it.

I'm not really ready to die.

Why should I die for them. All they want is a chance to get on with their selfish little imaginary little lives.

I'd die for my mates. Because we've earned it. As for the
rest of them. Living on in their kingdom of light with
their cities and their glorious pavements and their
freedom parades, walking on the dust that used to be us,
well they're laughing aren't they. I hate them. Maybe
it's not even worth hanging around if I just have to be
with them.

Available in *Faith*, published by Oberon Books Ltd. Reprinted
by kind permission of the publisher.

ISBN: 1 870259 80 7.

AUGUSTINE'S OAK

by Peter Oswald

Augustine's Oak was first performed at Shakespeare's Globe in August 1999. It was the first new play commissioned to be performed at this historic theatre.

This verse play concerns the conversion of Britain to Christianity in the Dark Ages by Saint Augustine. Aneirin is the link between the action and the audience, in the manner of the chorus in Shakespeare's Henry V. *Here he is describing a fierce battle on the Welsh border.*

Accent: *Welsh.*

ANEIRIN: I stood on a bright hillside looking to the east,
　　And at my feet the heather and the grass were tugged
　　By the blue infinite of space, and quietness was rife;
　　It was the windblown stillness of my country's thoughts,
　　The song no sword can end. Two walls of shields
　　　　　　　　　　　　　　　　　　　　　stepped out,
　　And with a shout of Jesus one ran to the other
　　That like a chalk cliff met the rush and turned it back
　　But let a few lumps slip that crashed into the wash,
　　Leaving green gaps – I saw the shrieking souls leap up
　　Like gulls by sudden updrifts caught and carried off,
　　And then the friends behind stepped forward and remade
　　The wall with their own selves, as April mends the world;
　　And for a while the air was humming like a lyre
　　With arrows and with spears that sped like thrushes, flung
　　To bury their sharp heads in earth or wood or men,
　　Looking for worms where worms would very soon be found;
　　And the opposing coasts collapsed into the waves,
　　And then the rain came down to wash the stained
　　　　　　　　　　　　　　　　　　　　　swords clean
　　That flashed above the press, among the animals
　　Head down in scarlet pools; the work of turning men
　　To earth was warmly and with good spades carried on,
　　And the blows came and went as fast as happy days.

But then a rainbow, stretched above the congregation,
Put heart into the Christians – they began an anthem
And suddenly the heathens scattered like blown sand.
This was the battle of the mud against the mud.
But now the slow crows croak, fold over in the sky,
And float to earth, wings spread and claws stretched
                                        out to grip
Whatever shows above the bog this mad herd churned,
And nature in her many secret processes,
Breaks the remains. The earth makes use of all our wars,
And never stops to stare or holds her breath in awe.

Available in *Augustine's Oak*, published by Oberon Books Ltd.
Reprinted by kind permission of the publisher.

ISBN: 1 84002 128 4.

NIJINSKY: DEATH OF A FAUN

by David Pownall

Nijinsky: Death Of A Faun was first performed at the Glynne Wickham Studio, Bristol University in May 1991.

The play is a one-person drama about the legendary dancer, Vaslav Nijinsky. It is set in the Bellevue Sanatorium in Switzerland where Nijinsky has been institutionalised because of his madness. Nijinsky was the star of the Ballets Russes, *and the lover of its creator, Serge Diaghilev. When Nijinsky married, without Diaghilev's permission, he was sacked from the* Ballets Russes. *Within three or four years, Nijinsky's mental health declined severely. The play is set in a bare room with a crucifix, in August 1920, when Nijinsky, aged 29, receives news of Diaghilev's death.*

Accent: *any.*

NIJINSKY: My madness, such as it is, seems to be limited these days to talking to myself, but, when I've got nothing to say I keep quiet which is an attitude that a lot of talkative people could learn from.

As for being withdrawn, well, there was a lot of pain which I didn't want to encounter again.

My wife has stuck me in here while she goes to America to lecture on how I used to dance. Sad, but we need the money.

The American government would not give me permission to enter the country. The American government does not allow mentally unsound people to enter the country. We need the money to keep me in here.

I am not mentally unsound. I am not my wife. I can dance.

I can lecture on dancing. I can earn money to keep me in here.

But I cannot lecture on how I *used* to dance. That is too sad.

My wife has left me here in this sanatorium. I will never get out.

My wife should be here in this sanatorium and I should be in America lecturing on dancing. My wife is a terrible dancer. Always was.

Doctor Binswanger says that there's money to be made in America.

The Stock Exchange on Wall Street is going mad but they are making money. I am mad but I am not making any money, stuck here.

My wife is afraid of poverty.

Today there is no god. There is only a piece of wood.

Piece of Wood, I intercede for Sergei Pavlovich Diaghilev.

He is not a villain for all time.

Just for the time he was with me.

I am Nijinsky, the leaper.

I leapt into bed with Prince Pavel Dmitrievich Lvov who passed me on to Sergei Pavlovich Diaghilev who passed me on to madness.

When madness tires of me he will pass me on to Tolstoy because Tolstoy has all the answers. Good old Tolstoy.

I am not permitted to read his books. *War and Peace* upset me.

I thought that was the idea.

Tolstoy knows nothing of poverty.

He gambles on the Stock Exchange but he writes well.

My wife comes from an aristocratic background.

She could lecture on flower arrangement but not dancing.

I am the dancer. I am the leaper. I am Nijinsky.

Available in *Nijinsky: Death of a Faun*, published by Oberon Books Ltd. Reprinted by kind permission of the publisher.

ISBN: 1 84002 000 8.

PART THREE: THIRTIES

TOAST

by Richard Bean

Toast was first performed at the Royal Court Theatre Upstairs in February 1999.

The play is set in 1975 and covers the Sunday night shift in a Yorkshire bread plant. Seven men come together to bake enough bread to feed the population of Hull. Robert Blakey is the chargehand. He wears baker's whites which have seen three or four shifts, and a striped office shirt with an open collar. He wears Buddy Holly black spectacles. His hair is mid-seventies style with sideburns. His sleeves are rolled up. He is a physical man, prone to bouncing on his feet and touching his crotch unnecessarily. He has tattoos on each forearm. He fantasises about being a rock 'n' roll performer. He is showing Lance, a mature student, around the plant – it is Lance's first night at work.

Accent: *Yorkshire.*

BLAKEY: (*Offering his hand.*) Blakey, Robert Blakey. This is Walter Nelson. Our mixer. (*Shakes hands.*) We work a six-day week. Nights is three till finish. Finish can be anywhere between eleven at night to three in't morning. Wednesdays and Thursdays we work a twelve-hour shift – seven at night till seven in't morning. Last day is Friday – three till finish again. That's a sixteen-hour day on Friday and maybe a few hours of Saturday morning thrown in. Then you're back here again Sunday morning at seven. How's that grab yer?

Is it legal? You get paid. Bit old for a student, aren't you? Let me see your hands. I gorra check for dermatitis.

BLAKEY takes LANCE's hands and turns them palms up. He sees LANCE has a scarred left wrist and pushes up LANCE's cuff for a better look at his wound.

If I were you I'd keep them cuffs rolled down like you had 'em. Our oven won't bite so hard that way.

BLAKEY goes to a cupboard and takes out two pairs of coarse sackcloth oven gloves, which he gives to LANCE.

Wear two pair of gloves. Last student we had lasted two hours. I had to tek him to infirmary mesen. Crying he was. Sociologist. Come with me, Sir Lancelot. I'm gonna put you on the oven. You ever seen a reel oven? It's not dangerous so long as you keep up with it, and don't panic when it gets ahead.

The phone rings. BLAKEY answers it.

(*On the phone.*) Bread plant…Yeah, it's me…Hello Mr Beckett, what's up…You wanna come in and do a shift?… Ha, ha! I'd treat yer well…Mmm…Mm…You what?… Are you pulling my plonker?…How many?…That'll tek us till four in the morning. How many again?…Wi' lids?…Right…Well, you could've told 'em to fuck off… Yeah, yeah, yeah, yeah…I know, if Bradford ses bek it we gorra bek it…They'll send an artic yeah?…Right, tarra.

(*He puts the phone down and turns to WALTER.*) Skeltons 'ave 'ad a fuck-up. Bradford are telling us to do three thousand for 'em. Big uns, aye. (*To LANCE.*) Huh, you're gonna 'ave some fun tonight sunshine.

Available in *Toast*, published by Oberon Books Ltd. Reprinted by kind permission of the publisher.

ISBN: 1 84002 104 7.

TOAST

by Richard Bean

See note on the play on page 55.

Lance is in his mid-thirties. He wears country tweeds and leather brogues, and a red rugby shirt with a white collar. His hair is collar-length and unkempt. He is a mature student of social and economic history, working his first shift at a Yorkshire bread plant. Here he is speaking to Walter, known as 'Nellie' – a broken man of 59. Lance is winding Nellie up – or is he?

Accent: *Yorkshire.*

LANCE: Would it be possible to touch you for a cigarette? I normally eschew the weed, on health grounds naturally, but in situations like this the pressure of social conformity is greater than my will to live. I'm using 'will to live' there as a figure of speech naturally – having raged unsuccessfully against the dying of the light several years ago.

I'm not a student Walter. I'm not at school. I'm here to see you. I can't tell you Walter, being dead has made a significant difference to my life. I have no concerns about my health, and I groom less. (*Beat.*) It is very opportune for me – being 'on a smoke' whilst you are taking your half-hour. Alone in the canteen. It is quite perfect. One might even say designed. I feared that I would have to corner you in the lavatory or steal thirty seconds in the mixing room, just to be with you.

Pause.

Are you prepared Walter?

That is exactly what I said! How can one prepare? Death is the only real adventure. Planning, preparation, making ready – all tosh! A willing acquiescence with fate is all that one can reasonably contribute. (*Beat.*) I have told them but they take very little notice of me. I said take him, snatch him away, suddenly. Why go to the expense of sending a messenger? Do you realise, Walter, to send me here has required eight signatures on two separate requisitions. One for the exceptional expenditure incurred, and one for a four-day visa.

Where am I from? The other side. From across the metaphorical water. No Walter, not Grimsby. The land of living souls and rotting bodies. The next world. I'm a messenger. Your time is up, Walter. They've made a decision at last. An all-night meeting. A compromise solution was suggested which, though not ideal, did not damage the long-term objectives of either party. There's a place for you now. Provision has been made. Your er… loyalty to this company, and all-round contribution to society, albeit in the narrow area of bread mass production, served you well. The committee actually calculated how many loaves you've mixed in the forty-five years you've worked here. Two hundred and twenty million. That's an awful lot of toast Walter. They're very pleased with you. All that bread! Ha! It's a mountain Walter! The decision, in the end, was unanimous – a very rare thing. The committee are already discussing the merits of another case. Walter, trust me, it's not as terrible as it sounds. I know where you're going. It's not perfect, but it could be worse. Let's just say, there are more ovens here – *comprenez*?

You are going to die Walter. Tonight. It'll be quick, and, thankfully, there'll be hardly any mess.

Available in *Toast*, published by Oberon Books Ltd. Reprinted by kind permission of the publisher.

ISBN: 1 84002 104 7.

DEAD MAN'S HANDLE

by John Constable

Dead Man's Handle was first performed by the Soho Theatre Company.

This short play is a three-hander, set in an intensive care unit where a man lies dying. The doctor is talking to the woman, who is in shock. The doctor hands her a glass of water.

Accent: *any*.

DOCTOR: It's okay…I don't mean…I mean I…I don't think…I don't think what you're going through is ever easy…for anyone. I have to say, I do think you're coping remarkably well.

But – oh, I think you are. But I think – I mean I don't think anyone can go through what you're going through and hold it all…you know…you've got to – got to – cry for him and…give yourself time to think it through – start to – come to terms…and I think it's good that – that's what you're starting to do. I do think…if we're going to – talk it through…I er…I think you'd better sit down.

He offers her the bedside chair. The WOMAN seems not to notice, staring at the MAN in bed. The DOCTOR coughs.

As I said, we're going to have to look at the scans in more detail. But – I'm afraid it does – does look as if there is very severe and extensive damage to his brain. Now, what this means…we can keep him alive, in a stable condition but…the fact is…that to all intents and purposes – the only things keeping his heart beating and – that sort of thing…are the drugs and the – the fact that he's on the ventilator.

The thing is…as things stand…the most we can do is – is to maintain him in some sort of – half-life. In this sense we – as doctors – we can't heal him…we're reduced to – we're really no more than…technicians…

I know it's hard – when you care for someone – even if they don't know you exist…it's – as if you – you somehow invest them with life. But – as I said – it does – does look as though the damage is irreversible. Okay?

I do think…we do have to – face the fact – he isn't going to get any better. Sooner or later I think we're going to have to – you know – to…think through some very hard…things…I think. Okay?

Available in *John Constable: Sha-Manic Plays*, published by Oberon Books Ltd. Reprinted by kind permission of the publisher.

ISBN: 1 870259 90 4.

THE FALSE HAIRPIECE

by John Constable

The False Hairpiece was first performed by Proteus Theatre Company.

The play is set on the Crow Farm somewhere in Hampshire. Jake, in his early thirties, is the "black sheep" of a farming family who has been in trouble with the law and confined in a mental institution. His therapist believes a lot of his problems stem from his relationship with his parents and he has come home to work these through, only to find his successful doctor brother, Charles, is present because their father has just died. Ma, his mother, makes Jake a bowl of soup. Jake is talking to both of them.

Accent: *Southern England.*

JAKE: He's dead, isn't he?

I thought so…

He thoughtfully resumes eating.

I had a feeling…(*Eats.*) Well, it was a bit more than a feeling actually. Da came to me. (*Eats.*) Ma, this is delicious. (*Stops in mid-mouthful.*) I'm sorry. Is this an inappropriate reaction? I'm never sure how to behave in moments like this. When Magic Ripley fell out of his tree at Newbury I couldn't stop laughing. I wouldn't want you to mistake my outward lack of emotional affect as indicative of lack of care with regard to Da.

He came to me in a dream. Well it was a bit more than

a dream, really, more like lucid dreaming – all part of the illuminations. He was there in his wheelchair, punching out the old phonemes on that voice-box of his, only no sound came out. It was like he was punching the messages straight into my brain – like all the data in this frolicking gynormous computer being downloaded into my brain – and I knew if I could just make sense of it…

He resumes eating. MA and CHARLES struggle to control their alarm and impatience.

And I couldn't. Couldn't process it. He told me everything I need to know, but I didn't know what to do with the information. Bear in mind, at the time in question, I was totally loop-de-loop.

What can you do? We knew it was only a matter of time. Suppose I'm too late for the funeral.

Available in *John Constable: Sha-Manic Plays*, published by Oberon Books Ltd. Reprinted by kind permission of the publisher.

ISBN: 1 870259 90 4.

THE DARKER FACE OF THE EARTH

by Rita Dove

See note on the play on page 27.

Amalia, wife of plantation owner Louis Jennings, has scandalously given birth to a half-caste child by one of the black slaves owned by her husband. The doctor is determined to hush it up, not just for the sake of the Jennings family, but for all white slaveowners in the district.

Accent: Southern.

DOCTOR: There he is. Now:
    I'll take the baby to Charleston tonight.
    You must play the wronged wife.
    No matter the truth – whatever the truth –
    this affair was an act of revenge,
    your retaliation to Louis' philandering.
    But you won't keep the child
    to taunt him, oh, no! Instead,
    you'll forgive and forget…and show him
    how to turn a profit besides.

    AMALIA stares at the DOCTOR in disgust. The DOCTOR opens the door.

    Come in, sir.

    LOUIS enters, glaring.

    This is a damned tricky situation,
    but I think I've sorted it out.

    Warming to his role as the arbiter of responsibility and morality; pacing self-importantly.

    Out of rage and sorrow over
    your philandering behaviour, Louis,
    Amalia has responded in kind.

An extreme vindication, true,
and utterly reprehensible – unless
we remember what prompted it
in the first place. Are we agreed?

Both LOUIS and AMALIA are silent.

As for the bastard child…

Pauses for effect.

Amalia has agreed to let it go.
I have a friend in Charleston
who likes raising slaves
from the ground up. He's familiar
with the story of the distraught wife
confronted with the evidence
of a husband's wandering lust.

No-one need know it's come from the Jennings Plantation.

We'll say the poor soul expired
directly after birth, took one breath
and died. I've taken the body away.
Amalia didn't want a funeral.
They'll believe it. They have no choice.

To AMALIA.

You better make sure the father
keeps his mouth shut.

Available in *The Darker Face of the Earth*, published by Oberon Books Ltd. Reprinted by kind permission of the publisher.

ISBN: 1 84002 129 2.

TOBACCOLAND

by Alex Finlayson

Tobaccoland was first performed at the Royal Exchange Theatre, Manchester, in April 1999.

The play concerns an elderly man, Hearon Smalls, and his feisty daughter, Vette, who run a tobacco farm in the hot dusty landscape of North Carolina. Vette has a half-cast son, Reno. Jim Sam is the local sheriff. He is black, a descendant of slaves who used to work for Hearon's grandfather. Reno is a wild child and here Jim Sam has decided to try to set him on the straight and narrow by giving him a piece of his mind.

Jim Sam pushes Reno through the double doors. Reno is handcuffed, but he never cowers or flinches. Jim Sam drops the ball.

Accent: *Black Southern American.*

JIM SAM: We're gonna have us some words fore I carry you up to the house. I don't wanta havta pick you up agin, boy. You wasted my time just about enough, so let's get this straight here and now –

JIM SAM backhands RENO across the face. When RENO's face twists back to JIM SAM it is the same look RENO always has.

(*Continuing.*) Is that what's it gonna take knock some sense into that nappy head of yours? Put it in the game, that's what I said. Get you some pussy. Go wide. But, no sir. No sir. Not gonna listen. We know what you are. They may be blind enough not to, but we see you, boy. We see your black ass. Your daddy was a nigger, boy. Just like me. And that makes you a nigger too. But you got you a way out, boy. You got you a future. So why you wanna go and blow it? Hangin with trash. Actin like trash. You got people up there give your ass anything. Every light in the house on up there. An a dining room suite laid out with the fatted calf. Good people for a nigger boy. White people. Your people. That old white man thinks you're sumpen special. He's gonna give all this to you. All this land. Land my granddaddy loved better'n his own blood. Slaved on. Shitted on. Prayed for. Land that'll go to the seed of a trashy white girl and a California no-name street nigger. Boy, you're the prodigal son! You just got to make up your mind, boy! You can eat with the swine or dine on the fatted calf. Make up your mind. Use that nappy head for some smartness, boy. Use it quick.

JIM SAM unlocks the handcuffs. He pulls RENO to his feet and straightens him. JIM SAM puts a kind hand on the boy's shoulder.

(*Continuing.*) There is joy in the presence of the angels of God over one sinner that repenteth. Let's get on up there and get us somethin to eat, boy.

Available in *Tobaccoland*, published by Oberon Books Ltd. Reprinted by kind permission of the publisher.

ISBN: 1 84002 085 7.

TOBACCOLAND

by Alex Finlayson

See note on the play on page 65.

Carter 'Pulley' Carter Smalls is the ne'er-do-well, thirty-something son of tobacco farmer Hearon. He has returned to the family farm in North Carolina after a period of wildness. Late at night, Pulley and his sister Vette have been laughing, drinking and talking over old times by a fire in the fields. Now he reveals why he has come back – his damaged relationship with his absent mother has been his excuse for failing to make anything of his life.

Accent: Southern American.

PULLEY: (*Takes a deep breath then plunges.*) I saw mom. Sug. She called me. An we met. For lunch. This place in Charlotte, fancy ladies' lunch place, in my work clothes, and I've got 45 minutes max, and she comes in, and I didn't even know who she was. I didn't recognise my own mother. She's blonde – or that kind of, you know, rich women hair. And she had some pretty interesting stuff to say. I mean, stuff you might want to hear. Sometime.

I'm gonna see her again, Vette. She wants to see you. And she wants to see Reno. We've got three half-brothers. I've been waitin a long time. Just to find out. I don't know… She tried.

There were letters. Musta been hundreds of'm, she said. (*Now the words come tumbling out as if PULLEY were nine years old.*) Cuz she wrote all the time, and she thought we were gettin the letters, just that he wudden lettin us write back. She knew the first year they were married she'd made a mistake cuz Daddy was so weird when they came back here, around grandaddy, an, an how they argued about him workin us in the fields like, like…

An her freakin out watching Ludie and Nella in the field
bitin the heads off tobacco worms, spittin'm out, laughin
She'd never seen anything like that. An' Daddy startin
drinkin, you know, and all his other bullshit stuff. She
tried, Vette. I promise she did.

Available in *Tobaccoland*, published by Oberon Books Ltd.
Reprinted by kind permission of the publisher.

ISBN: 1 84002 085 7.

SAD HOTEL

by David Foley

Sad Hotel was first performed in 1998.

The play is a fictionalised account of the relationship between Tennessee Williams and his lover, Frank Merlo. Set in a house on the Florida coast in the early 1960s, Tom (the Williams character) is a flamboyant alcoholic homosexual who makes huge emotional demands on all who love him. Frank is a short, handsome, compact man in his early forties. He has been Tom's faithful companion, secretary and lover for 15 years. Now a handsome 19-year-old Cuban, Pedro, has been brought into the household and it seems Frank is to be replaced by him. He is speaking to Pedro.

Accent: *American.*

FRANK: Clean the house. Pay the bills. Drive the car. Buy the food and the detergent and the toilet paper. Cook. Keep track of his appointments and his engagements and the promises he's made in his nightly drunken haze. Find the things he's lost and remind him of what he's forgotten. Pack his suitcases. Unpack them. Pack them up again. Maintain an idea – a dim semblance of home in one house, two apartments, and a thousand hotel rooms in the long blur of cities and faces and unremembered incidents your life will become.

That's the easy part.

Now hold his hand. I said hold it!

Roughly, he puts TOM's hand in PEDRO's and holds them together.

You feel that thing coursing into your arm? That's the Panic. You'll learn to live with the Panic.

You'll learn to recognise it, when it comes on without warning, when night has fallen sooner than expected and suddenly whatever room you've landed in has gone dark

and empty – except for the two of you. So hold his hand.
Hold it and tell him he's not dying or failing or losing
his mind. Tell him he's not alone and won't die alone,
like his father, in some rented room, in some strange
city, in the middle of the night.

After a while you'll lose the sense of where his panic
ends and yours begins, and then you'll find that you've
started taking a few things yourself to keep the spooks
away: a few pills now and then or a shot of something
strong, something to get you both through those long,
long nights…when you no longer have the strength to
hold the both of you up alone…

Pause.

I don't know…if it's worth it. I can't…advise you.
I haven't figured it out myself yet. But it will be easier,
I think, if you don't love him. I don't know for sure, but
yes, I think it would be easier, if you didn't love him.

Good luck. (*Exiting right.*) Good night.

Available in *Sad Hotel*, published by Oberon Books Ltd.
Reprinted by kind permission of the publisher.

ISBN: 1 84002 085 7.

THE SNOW PALACE

by Pam Gems

The Snow Palace was first performed at the Wilde Theatre, Bracknell in January 1998 and subsequently at the Tricycle Theatre, Kilburn after a national tour.

Poland in the 1920s. In a freezing wooden hut the writer Stanislawa Przybyszewska lives alone as she writes her epic play, The Danton Affair, *about the rivalry and jockeying for power of Danton and Robespierre during the French Revolution. Her morphine addiction causes the characters to come to life in her head, and in her hut. Here Robespierre is at the Paris Tribunal, fighting for his own survival and the destruction of his enemy, Danton. Robespierre is a fanatic and an idealist, more excited by ideas than by emotions.*

Accent: received pronunciation

ROBESPIERRE: (*Shrill, against the noise.*) I request the right to speak…I request the right to speak! (*He stands, immobile, waits a long time for the noise to die down.*)

(*Mildly.*) It's a long time, gentlemen, since we began our sitting with such a display of temper. (*He pauses, looks around.*) Today…today we shall see what we value more – the Republic – or the individual.

Citizen Legendre demands that the accused be allowed to answer charges from this floor. (*Shouts of agreement. He raises his voice.*) Are you saying – are you saying that you wish to accord to those now under arrest privileges that have been denied those preceding them? If Citizen Legendre believes in special consideration then that is a mistake which we must correct in him. It is not the function of a revolutionary Convention to grant privilege. That is what we are here to abolish.

Gentlemen – what are we here for? We are here to create a new society. A society based on the notion of democracy. On the notion of personal freedom – (*A sudden scream.*) No man is born a slave! Another man makes him so! (*Some cheering. He recovers his coolness.*) We mean to build a state without hierarchy, where notions of comfort, dignity and personal happiness are not confined to the few at the expense of the many. You think that impossible? With so much energy locked in want and despair? Wasted in human beings deprived of the means of survival, let alone education, civilisation! I tell you, we have the means to unlock that energy. Here, for the first time in the history of the world, we have a chance to save the world, for the world…for the people of the world…ALL people…everywhere! Must that great work be put at risk? For personal greed? For criminality? I, Maximilien Robespierre – Citizen – say NO!!! (*Cheers.*)

I move that the order for the arrest of the prisoner Danton and his confederates be confirmed.

Available in *The Snow Palace*, published by Oberon Books Ltd. Reprinted by kind permission of the publisher.

ISBN: 1 84002 065 2.

SOUNDS…IN SESSION

by Tyrone Huggins

See note on the play on page 35.

Nic Forcast is white and middle-aged. He once owned an independent record label before selling out to a mega-bucks commercial label reduced him to producing cheesy disco hits. He needs the credibility of a commercial hit if he's to escape being a has-been. He is talking to singer Sandra and sound engineer Tony.

Accent: any.

NIC: In demo world music is more than just making squiggly sounds. It's Rock and Roll, it's Blues, it's Jazz, Soul, R&B, Classical – it's popular music – real life! I used to be a roadie. When being on the road was the back of a freezing Transit, with the hi-hat stand poking up your arse. Played a gig in Brodie's Bar, Edinburgh, really stomping night. De-rigged, loaded up, got some beers in to take to the flat. The band got there first, of course, taken all the beds. The sound engineer and me were left with sleeping bags on the floor – they get the glamour, we get the crick in the neck. Just got off to sleep when Susie, the singer, came running in, shrieking – just like she sang – 'there's a man killing a woman out on the streets!' As if it was any of my business. Half asleep dragged my jeans on – no shoes – ran down five flights of stairs out the front of that tenement to see this couple. Man's got hold of her face, she's got his hair scratching like a vixen yelling murder at each other; 'why don't you kill me then go on kill me why don't you kill me!' She's shouting over and over. And he's shouting, 'shut up, shut up…you want me to kill you, shut up!' And I'm witnessing this, 'why don't you kill me!' And I say hang on, cool it you two, cool it, let her go mate, or something equally foolish. Next thing I know he's turned on me. 'Who the fuck are you? What

the fuck's it got to do with you?' And he lets her go.
Splat! Right on the nose. Blood. Like Rocky. Then she's
coming scratching and kicking and screaming, at me
now. In a daze, blood on me Buzzcocks T-shirt,
I stumble back to the door of the block. I've locked
myself out. There's an array of doorbells swimming out
of focus in front of me – I don't know which flat we're
in! In me bare feet, freezing. (*Pause.*) After waking half
the block I get back inside, they're carrying on; 'why
don't you kill me then go on kill me!' Susie's back in
bed, fast asleep. Life, as lived by real people.
I learned about passion that night. (*Pause.*) Never come
between other people's passion.

Available in *Sounds...In Session*, published by Oberon Books
Ltd. Reprinted by kind permission of the publisher.

ISBN: 1 84002 096 2.

PLAYING SINATRA

by Bernard Kops

See note on the play on page 37.

Norman, an agoraphobic bookbinder with an obsessive, exclusive relationship with his sister Sandra, is trying to make her see that the man she has brought into their lives, Phillip, is a con man. It is Norman's birthday.

Accent: any.

NORMAN: Sandra darling. Let's start the party now. Please. We have to wait for no-one. That trifle looks too inviting.

(*He sits down, puts on a paper hat, smiles, leans across and puts one on her head.*) Let's start, please. I love just the two of us. (*He starts to sing 'Happy Birthday'.*) Sandra, I don't want people. I have no vacancies. I am all full up with people. Take some trifle. Don't wanna wait.

I don't think he'll be coming. (*Ending his song.*) Happy birthday to me. Who is this Phillip? Where did he come from? We know nothing about him. (*Singing to the tune 'Who Is Silvia'.*) 'Who is Phillip? What is he? That comes from outer darkness…' Sorry. If he were the good King Arthur I would fear him. I fear any stranger except Mr Frank Sinatra, but then, he's no stranger.

(*Quietly.*) Sandra! Five thousand pounds withdrawn? Yesterday? Look! This is an entry in your own little Building Society book. There! Five thousand pounds withdrawn. What have you done with the money? Or did Minerva cost that much? Has your love for me gone completely overboard? (*Now heavy.*) WHAT HAVE YOU DONE WITH THE MONEY? (*He holds her wrists, is hurting her.*) Tell me or I swear I'll murder you. What have you done with that money?

Darling! Please!

Sandra, you and I – we don't have a separate existence. If we are not us who are we then? What have all the years meant? Nothing? Am I nothing? I feel so sorry for you.

I've had enough. Think I need you? All my life you've used me as an excuse for your own fears, because you think you're as ugly as a turd. But now you've gone too far.

Not interested. Sorry Sandra. Argument over. Let's be friends. (*He goes to the table, eats voraciously.*) Try some of these cakes. They're absolutely scrumptious. Mmmmm! Sandra, I'm saying this in the nicest possible way, in a spirit of conciliation. You fell for the oldest trick in the world. You of all people. You fell for a pathetic con man, didn't you? You just gave him that money. Admit! Admit. Anyway, it's not really your fault. That's the whole point about con men; they're so believable.

Available in *Bernard Kops: Plays One*, published by Oberon Books Ltd. Reprinted by kind permission of the publisher.

ISBN: 1 84002 071 7.

THE DRAMATIC ATTITUDES
OF MISS FANNY KEMBLE

by Claire Luckham

The Dramatic Attitudes of Miss Fanny Kemble was first performed at the Nuffied Theatre, Southampton in November 1990.

The play concerns the adventures of a nineteenth-century actress and darling of the West End stage, Fanny Kemble, who fell in love with and married a wealthy American landowner, Pierce Butler. Pierce owns plantations and therefore slaves, and he is greatly distressed and his life upset when his new wife takes the side of the slaves over her husband's interests. Here he is trying to make Fanny "see sense" about the slaves.

Accent: *Southern American.*

PIERCE: Imagine any damn thing you like! You're an actress, Fanny, you are trained to use your imagination in the theatre, on stage. There's no place for all this feverish imagining in real life. I've got to run this place – and run this place I will, with or without your help.

You're making my job practically impossible. Dramatising everything, the whole damn time. You can't help it. It's in your blood.

Go on, make a scene, make me feel like a worm. I've attacked the precious family.

I am sick to death with you and your imagination. People have dogs that they imagine are human. I like dogs, and their owners can be my best friends. But a dog is a dog. They only think they are human because they spend all their time giving them human characteristics; reading all manner of bosh into a doggy nature, simply because the blasted dog can't answer back. I mean the dog would say it was a dog if it could! It is the same – you think that they can't talk to you on your level because they haven't got the culture, rather the education. But we have education, letters, music, art – culture – because we're white. It's happened because we've made it happen.

I am a practical person, and I know that the only way to deal with my slaves is to treat them in a disciplined, sensible manner. While you! I can't have you going around treating them as though they were martyrs, some kind of superior being.

Frightened? I'm not frightened. Look, Fanny, I've given you everything you've asked for. I'm loving, understanding, generous – to a fault. All I'm asking is that you stay out of this. Frightened? What the hell of?

I'm going to change for dinner before you say anything else. This is absurd.

Available in *Luckham: Plays*, published by Oberon Books Ltd. Reprinted by kind permission of the publisher.

ISBN: 1 870259 68 8.

THE SEDUCTION OF ANNE BOLEYN

by Claire Luckham

The Seduction of Anne Boleyn was first performed at the Nuffield Theatre, Southampton in April 1998.

The play is a fresh look at the history of the relationship between King Henry VIII and his second wife, Anne Boleyn. Henry divorced his first wife, Katherine of Aragon, after twenty years of marriage when she was unable to provide him with a male heir. This caused a split with the Catholic Church and triggered the Reformation. Henry subsequently married Anne Boleyn, but she too failed to bear him a male child and he had her executed on the grounds of adultery with her brother and with a young musician. In this scene, Henry confronts Anne with her "inability" to bear him an heir. He is a handsome man still, in the prime of life.

Accent: received pronunciation

HENRY: One daughter, one miscarriage and now another loss. Lost. Another loss – Anne? Why? We know Katherine's babies died because God couldn't bless us. Our marriage was an abomination. Then why was this child born dead? What's wrong with our marriage? Did you see him? They told me that he was malformed. Malformed? What does that mean? How can a child of mine be anything but perfect? Did you see him? Did they show him to you? What was wrong with him? How was he imperfect? My son? You do know what this signifies? God is angry. Who with? You? Me? A blasted child is the result of some filthy thing. Why should God damn us? I flirted – only. This is not because I flirted. You cannot lay the blame for this at my feet. He doesn't judge me. Not his servant, no. Through me he breathes. Perhaps you've forgotten that my authority comes from him? He blesses me. So how can I be the one at fault?

There are two explanations for this: either you cannot
give me sons because you are somewhere deep down
inside unwholesome, a cesspit, a stinking trough of evil.
God knows, I've had to listen to enough people telling
me that you have enchanted me; in simple terms –
you are a witch. I scorned them. Tell me, isn't it true
that witches are unable to bear male children? And isn't
it also true that they can affect a man's performance
in bed? You know how hard that child was to conceive.
What am I to believe? That I have been put under
a spell?

The second explanation for this debacle and the one
I prefer, is that poor blighted babe was not my son.
I was not the father. He was the product of some sin,
some licentious thing, some disgusting adultery – such
as witches perform with the devil. You were, have been
unfaithful to me.

Available in *Luckham: Plays* published by Oberon Books Ltd.
Reprinted by kind permission of the publisher.

ISBN: 1 870259 68 8.

YO-YO

by Dino Mahoney

See note on the play and plot outline on page 15.

Kevin, a divorced schoolteacher, has arrived in Cornwall expecting to spend some time with his infant son, Ben. Kevin is aged 30, a secondary school teacher working in London. He has working class origins, and is university educated. Kevin's life is invaded by Lego, a troubled 14-year-old boy, who is determined to gain his attention. Their relationship develops in unexpected directions as both man and boy discover some sense of kindred with each other. Kevin is talking to Lego.

Accent: London.

KEVIN: (*Spluttering with laughter.*) I don't know. I have nothing to laugh about Lego…nothing. (*He again splutters with laughter.*) It's hysteria, take no notice…(*He drinks.*) I was doing volcanoes once.

There I was at the blackboard…coloured chalks…sound effects…(*Mimes chalking up an erupting volcano with appropriate sound effects.*) all accompanied by a riveting commentary on the earth's pent up energies…the trapped lava seething below the earth's crust…gripping stuff… then all aglow I turn around and see this slob in the front row sprawling at his desk with a lolly rammed down his throat, the stick poking out of his mouth…so I grab it and pull.

It was like yanking the pin out of a hand grenade. He put his fist through the door…it had glass panels in it… reinforced glass, you know the kind…chicken wire in it …well, it's that kind of school, they reinforced the glass in case someone put their fist through it…it's what you call…foresight. (*Pause.*) Should have been my face.

Was I scared? For him, yes…for me? I think so.

We're all nutters Lego, all of us. (*He drinks.*) Went home
with bloodstains on my jacket…it looked as if I worked
in an abattoir…and sometimes I think I do.

What I do isn't really teaching Lego…it's more like
surviving. When the morning bell goes everything
human goes with it. They don't know me…I'm someone
else…someone in their way…a policeman…a parent…
a schoolteacher…and they swear at me, insult me, ignore
me…until now I hate them back. It's pathetic.

Teach in a posh school? Ah yes…leave your ideals on
the pavement Sir and step inside…no, they wouldn't
have me Lego…not after seven years in the hole I've
been teaching in.

Available in *Yo-Yo,* published by Oberon Books Ltd. Reprinted
by kind permission of the publisher.

ISBN: 1 870259 50 5.

AUGUSTINE'S OAK

by Peter Oswald

See note on the play on page 47.

King Ethelbert of Britain is talking to his daughter, Tata. Ethelbert's wife has converted to Christianity and is now refusing to have anything to do with him until he does the same.

Accent: any.

ETHELBERT: We'll never find another chaplain like old Lethard. He understood me, you see. We could talk, he and I. A wonderful man, interested in everything. He talked about the things I like to talk about.

Lethard would say to your mother, I'm going to have a bit of a chat with the king, and go off, and she'd drop to her knees and pray every instant of the time she knew he was with me; Lethard would turn up wherever I was and we'd drink and sit talking about politics or hunting almost till dawn, then when I saw her she'd say, did you have a good talk with Lethard and I'd smile thoughtfully and reply, very interesting indeed; and she'd think I was making progress.

Why it should be a condition of entry to her secret heart that I believe in Jesus Christ, I can't see. I am her husband. Couldn't I say I do? Ah but it wouldn't be enough for me to whisper in her ear, love I believe. I'd have to be publicly baptised. And anyway it's her heart I want and I couldn't go creeping into that dressed in feathers.

This is far too complex for a king of my race. I imagine they suffer from such intrigues in Byzantium and Paris, but with us things ought to be clear and simple. Do I tear my hair out and weep because she won't believe in Woden, for heaven's sake?

Don't say that's gobbledygook. If your grandmother was here! Which she is! Ah, dear dear dear. Woden, don't listen.

You can't outwit the one-eyed one. Consider, Tata, my dear – his horse has eight legs. It takes him to the land of the dead and back in a night. He has drunk from Mimir's spring, he gave one eye in exchange for a sip; now he knows everything. He can nod to Freya and you will never have any children, your husband will lose his mind and stab you to death in bed when you are pregnant. Or he can nod to Thor and the hammer of disaster will fall smash on this kingdom, distribute our people as slaves to all comers. He can wink at Frey – close his only eye – and the wheat will wither. He can stare through the sky and on the day of battle turn me into a bird, chirping and flapping – all these things have happened, and continually happen, and not without reason because, my darling, Woden, the mad one, is in command. Fear him!

Available in *Augustine's Oak,* published by Oberon Books Ltd. Reprinted by kind permission of the publisher.

ISBN: 1 84002 128 4.

ROOM TO LET

by Paul Tucker

Room to Let was first performed at the Chelsea Theatre Centre in May 1999.

The play is set in the living room of a terraced house that has not been decorated in years. Eddie and Janet are an ordinary couple, in their fifties, enjoying simple daily pleasures. Then they take in a lodger – Roger. Roger is 33, from Swansea in South Wales. He is dressed in a feathery ginger-blond wig and a cheap second-hand sweater tucked into ill-fitting Farah hopsack trousers which are short in length. He wears eighties winklepickers with white socks. All this is topped off with a Swansea FC tattoo on one forearm and 'Mother' on the other. Together with the tinted glasses and the moustache, he thinks he's cool and trendy, the man about town. Roger is, in fact, Eddie's son from a previous marriage. Eddie abandoned them when Roger was a small baby. Here, Roger confronts Eddie about the pain he has caused.

Accent: *South Wales.*

ROGER: You'll never be able to make up for what you've done. At school, the kids called me a bastard, I used to dread it, walking through those big black metal gates in the morning where they would be waiting for me, the sky would be yellow and grey and you wunt believe how low I was for a nine-year-old. They would tear my hood off my coat or hit me with their belts when the teacher wasn't there, or they'd gob in my face or make me lie in dogshit, if they didn't call me a bastard, they called me flea bag or lurgy or leper. Mum couldn't afford new clothes so I never told her about the rips in my trousers or in my coat, I would sit in my bedroom and sew them up myself. Every day, I thought you might come back, I would imagine you walk up that garden path and you'd look up and see me at the bedroom window and as you'd come through that front door, things would be normal

again. The sun would come back, Christmas would be
a time to look forward to and I would never have to hear
mam crying downstairs all the time and listening to that
song every five minutes. But you never came did you?
You never walked up that path did you? You just walked
right out of our lives, gone, as if you never existed, as if
we didn't either. I wanted to find you, I wanted to see
what you had to say, it was heart-breaking to watch her
die, it killed me Eddie, it really fucking killed me. And
where were you? You weren't by her bedside, you weren't
holding her hand, you weren't telling her everything's
gonna be okay and God'll look after her. But the more
hurt I felt then, the more I would make you pay, and
now I don't have to cry any more. Because it's your turn
now, Eddie, it's your turn to do the crying.

Available in *Room to Let,* published by Oberon Books Ltd.
Reprinted by kind permission of the publisher.

ISBN: 1 84002 125 X.

Also published by Oberon Books in association with LAMDA:

Contemporary Scenes for Young Women (1985-2000)
ISBN: 1 84002 130 6

Solo Speeches for Men (1800-1914)
ISBN: 1 84002 046 6

Solo Speeches for Women (1800-1914)
ISBN:1 84002 003 2

First Folio Speeches for Men
ISBN: 1 84002 015 6

First Folio Speeches for Women
ISBN: 1 84002 014 8

Classics for Teenagers
ISBN: 1 84002 023 7

Scenes for Teenagers
ISBN: 1 84002 031 8

Solo Speeches for Under 12s
ISBN: 1 84002 013 X

The LAMDA Anthology of Verse and Prose, Vol XV
ISBN: 1 84002 120 9

The LAMDA Guide to English Literature
ISBN: 1 84002 011 3

The Discussion
ISBN: 1 870259 71 8

Mime and Improvisation
ISBN: 1 84002 012 1

Meaning, Form and Performance
ISBN: 1 870259 74 2